Wise Insight: Navigating the Waters of the Mind in a Manipulative World

Preface

In an increasingly connected world, where the lines between reality and fiction blur, there arises an urgent need for understanding and defense against an invisible yet powerful foe: mental manipulation. This book, titled "Wise Insight: Navigating the Waters of the Mind in a Manipulative World," is a comprehensive and enlightening guide for all those who wish to preserve their mental integrity in an often dark and complex landscape.

The importance of this topic cannot be underestimated. Through these pages, we invite you to embark on a journey of self-exploration, learning, and personal growth. Mental manipulation is a widespread phenomenon that can manifest in many forms, from personal relationships to the digital sphere, and awareness is the key to self-protection.

The book opens with an Introduction that lays the groundwork for mental manipulation, exploring the devastating effects it can have on the lives of its victims. Through a deep understanding of the psychological mechanisms involved, the second chapter outlines the various forms of mental manipulation, providing a useful map for navigating dangerous emotional terrain.

Often, early signs of manipulation escape our attention. In the third chapter, we tackle the challenge of recognizing manipulative behaviors and identifying at-risk situations, providing practical tools to develop early awareness. The next chapter delves into the psychology of the manipulator, exploring the psychological profile of those seeking to exert control over others and the power dynamics that guide them.

Individual vulnerability, a central theme of the fifth chapter, is carefully examined, encouraging thoughtful reflection on our weaknesses and how they can be exploited. On the flip side, the sixth chapter offers a positive perspective, presenting strategies to build mental resilience and develop emotional awareness.

Active prevention is the focus of the seventh chapter, where strategies to avoid manipulation situations are explored, emphasizing the importance of digital awareness education. The book continues with an in-depth look at psychological defenses in the eighth chapter, offering practical techniques and advice on establishing healthy boundaries in relationships.

The ninth chapter introduces self-analysis tools, with guiding questions to explore one's emotions and beliefs, allowing the reader to create a clear picture of their identity. Following chapters address care and recovery after manipulation experiences and the importance of community and positive relationships as antidotes to manipulation.

The book culminates in the thirteenth chapter, "Looking to the Future," where an optimistic view of life after the experience of manipulation is explored, along with the ongoing development of mental resilience. Finally, the Conclusion summarizes the key points covered and encourages the reader to share the acquired knowledge, cultivate healthy relationships, and contribute to awareness education.

"Wise Insight" is more than a book; it is a practical and inspiring guide for those who wish to navigate the complex terrain of the human mind with wisdom and discernment. Through awareness, education, and action, we hope this book can be a valuable resource for all those seeking a more authentic, resilient, and mindful life.

Chapter 1: Introduction

Contextualizing the Importance of the Topic

In the vast landscape of psychology and human relationships, few themes are as crucial and pervasive as that of mental manipulation. The subtle art of influencing an individual's thoughts and behavior, undermining their autonomy and authenticity, quietly seeps into the deepest fabrics of society. Mental manipulation knows no socio-economic, cultural, or geographical boundaries; it is a universal phenomenon that can affect anyone, regardless of their resilience or awareness.

In an era where we are immersed in an ocean of information and interconnections, mental manipulation manifests in increasingly sophisticated ways. Digital technologies and social media amplify the potential for manipulation, making it a tangible risk in each of our lives. The growing complexity of human relationships, both online and offline, has made it essential to understand and proactively address this phenomenon.

Our society, despite being characterized by progress and innovation, is permeated by subtle and dark forces that undermine the very fabric of trust and personal integrity. Mental manipulation takes various forms: from interpersonal relationships to the political sphere, from deceptive advertising to complex family dynamics. Recognizing the importance of this topic is the fundamental first step in building a society based on values of truth, respect, and awareness.

Brief Overview of the Effects of Mental Manipulation

The effects of mental manipulation are insidious and

can permeate every aspect of an individual's life. Whether occurring on a personal or collective level, manipulation can leave deep scars on the human psyche. Victims of manipulation often experience a sense of disorientation, a distortion of self-perception and perception of others, and sometimes a loss of confidence in their decision-making abilities.

Emotionally, manipulation can generate anxiety, depression, and a constant sense of insecurity. Victims may find themselves trapped in a cycle of self-doubt or toxic relationships, unable to discern reality from the manipulation endured. Socially, manipulation can undermine mutual trust, compromising the building of healthy relationships and the functioning of society as a whole.

Addressing the effects of mental manipulation requires a deep understanding of the dynamics involved and a commitment to promoting individual and collective awareness and resilience. This book aims to be a comprehensive guide for anyone who wishes not only to understand the phenomenon of mental manipulation but also to learn practical tools to defend themselves, heal, and contribute to a culture that promotes truth and authenticity. Through an enlightening perspective and effective practices, we will embark on a journey toward a richer, more secure, and conscious life, shattering the invisible chains of mental manipulation.

Chapter 2: Understanding Mental Manipulation

Definition and Types of Mental Manipulation

Definition

Mental manipulation, in all its forms, emerges as a subtle art of exerting psychological control over an individual, influencing their thoughts, emotions, and decisions in a subtle and not always evident manner. It is a violation of individual freedom, often operated through deceptive and manipulative tactics aimed at gaining the victim's consent or conformity without their conscious agreement.

Manipulation can manifest in different ways, ranging from emotional persuasion to information control, systematic denial of reality to the creation of psychological dependence. Understandable only through a multidimensional lens, mental manipulation is a complex phenomenon that requires an in-depth approach to be adequately recognized and addressed.

Types of Mental Manipulation

Emotional Manipulation:

- Exploits the victim's emotions to gain control.

- Involves creating situations that generate anxiety, guilt, or fear.

Cognitive Manipulation:

- Distorts the perception of reality through misleading or omitted information.

- Induces the victim to see only one side of the truth.

Social Manipulation:

- Uses social pressure or isolation to control the victim.

- May include threats or blackmail to influence behavior.

Narcissistic Manipulation:

- Focuses on increasing the power and control of the manipulating individual.

- Often involves manipulating the victim's self-esteem.

Technological Manipulation:

- Exploits technology and communication channels to manipulate opinions and behaviors.

- Includes spreading false information and creating

an "echo chamber."

Analysis of Involved Psychological Mechanisms

Mental manipulation draws from a wide range of psychological mechanisms that exploit human weaknesses and vulnerabilities. Some of these mechanisms include:

Gaslighting:

- Involves making the victim doubt their own perception of reality.

- Minimizes or denies obvious facts to confuse and destabilize.

Psychological Conditioning:

- Uses positive or negative reinforcements to shape desired behavior.

- Can create psychological dependence on gratification or fear of consequences.

Persuasion Techniques:

- Exploits emotional persuasion, authority, or scarcity of resources to influence decisions.

- Can occur through speeches, advertising, or social situations.

Emotional Isolation:

- Separation of the victim from friends, family, or external support.

- Makes the victim more dependent on the manipulating individual.

**Exploitation of Individual
Weaknesses:**

- Identification and
  exploitation of the victim's
  fears, insecurities, or
  desires.

- Adaptation of tactics
  based on specific
  vulnerabilities.

Understanding these mechanisms
is crucial for developing an
effective defense against mental
manipulation. As we continue
through this book, we will explore
how to recognize these tactics,
develop awareness, and adopt
strategies to protect our minds
and authenticity.

Chapter 3: Early Signs of Manipulation

Recognizing Manipulative Behaviors

The crucial first step in defending against mental manipulation is developing the ability to recognize early signs of manipulative behaviors. These signs may be subtle, but awareness of them is essential to preserve one's autonomy and integrity. Here are some common manipulative behaviors to watch out for:

Excessive Flattery:

- Excessive flattery can conceal manipulative intentions, creating emotional dependency.

Excessive Control:

- The need to control every aspect of the victim's life

can be a sign of manipulation.

Guilt and Shame:

- Manipulation often involves making the victim feel guilty or ashamed to gain compliance.

Sudden Behavior Changes:

- Sudden changes in attitude can indicate intentional manipulation to confuse the victim.

Veiled Threats:

- The use of subtle threats can make the victim feel vulnerable, prompting obedience for self-preservation.

Social Isolation:

- Separation from a support network is a sign of

manipulation, as it reduces opportunities for confrontation and resistance.

Lack of Respect for Boundaries:

- Ignoring personal boundaries is a common manipulative tactic to invade emotional space.

Information Manipulation:

- Providing selective or false information to influence the perception of reality.

Extreme Emotions:

- Using extreme emotions such as anger or desperation to elicit a specific behavior from the victim.

Identifying At-Risk Situations

Recognizing at-risk situations is equally important as identifying manipulative behaviors. Some situations may predispose individuals to the onset of mental manipulation:

Imbalanced Relationships:

- Power or control disparities in relationships can create fertile ground for manipulation.

Highly Competitive Environments:

- Excessive competition can lead to manipulations to gain personal advantages.

Ambiguity or Uncertainty:

- Situations with low clarity and certainty can be exploited to manipulate perception.

Stress and Individual Vulnerability:

- Periods of stress or vulnerability can make people more susceptible to manipulation.

Assertions of Unquestionable Authority:

- Situations where authority is accepted without critical reflection can facilitate manipulation.

Financial or Emotional Dependency:

- Dependency on a person or situation can increase vulnerability to manipulation.

Social Isolation:

- Lack of strong social connections can make it challenging to seek external advice on potentially manipulative situations.

Recognizing these signs and at-risk situations provides an anchor of awareness and allows for a timely response. As we continue reading, we will explore concrete strategies to prevent and effectively counteract mental manipulation, ensuring a comprehensive approach to safeguarding one's psyche.

Chapter 4: The Psychology of the Manipulator

Psychological Profile of Those Who Practice Manipulation

The manipulator, with their skillful use of subtle tactics, infiltrates relational dynamics by exploiting the weaknesses and vulnerabilities of their victims. Understanding the psychological profile of those who practice manipulation is essential to recognize early signs and adopt effective defense strategies.

Selective Empathy:

- The manipulator may display apparent empathy, but it is often selective and used only when it serves their purposes.

Charisma and Persuasion:

- Often endowed with magnetic charisma, the manipulator knows how to persuade and influence others with ease.

Lack of Genuine Empathy:

- Unlike an empathetic person, the manipulator does not genuinely feel compassion for others.

Narcissism:

- Many manipulators exhibit narcissistic traits, focused on the pursuit of power and recognition.

Seduction Skills:

- Uses emotional and psychological seduction to gain the compliance of victims.

Social Adaptability:

- Adapts adeptly to different situations, shaping their behavior according to circumstances.

Motivations and Power Dynamics

Motivations of the Manipulator

Control and Domination:

- The thirst for control is a fundamental motivation; the manipulator seeks to dominate others to satisfy their ego.

Self-Gratification:

- Manipulation can be fueled by the constant pursuit of personal gratification, regardless of the effects on victims.

Lack of Empathy:

- The lack of genuine empathy allows the manipulator to act without remorse toward victims.

Self-Affirmation:

- Manipulation often arises from the need to assert one's superiority or competence.

Power Dynamics

Creation of Dependency:

- The manipulator seeks to make victims dependent on them, generating a cycle of control and submission.

Social Isolation:

- Reduces the victim's support network, thus

increasing their power and control over the situation.

Information Manipulation:

- Controls and manipulates information to influence the victims' perception of reality.

Psychological Games:

- Entraps victims in psychological games, exploiting their emotional vulnerability to achieve the desired outcome.

Positive/Negative Reinforcement:

- Uses positive or negative reinforcement to shape the behavior of victims and ensure their own advantage.

Understanding the psychology of the manipulator is crucial for developing the resilience necessary against their tactics. As we proceed, we will explore practical strategies to protect oneself and maintain integrity in potentially manipulative situations.

Chapter 5: Individual Vulnerability

Factors Increasing Vulnerability to Manipulation

Psychological manipulation finds fertile ground in certain individual conditions and contexts. Understanding the factors that increase individual vulnerability is essential for developing critical awareness and effective defense.

Low Self-Esteem:

- Individuals with low self-esteem are more inclined to seek approval and acceptance, making them easier targets for the manipulator.

Need for Affection and Belonging:

- The desperate search for affection and belonging can lead to greater susceptibility to manipulation.

Personal Uncertainty:

- Uncertainty about one's beliefs or goals can facilitate manipulation by creating false reference points.

Fear of Conflict:

- Individuals who avoid conflict may easily yield to the manipulator's demands to maintain peace.

Emotional or Financial Dependency:

- Those dependent on someone or something are more susceptible to manipulation, as the manipulator can threaten to deprive them of what they depend on.

Lack of Knowledge about Manipulation:

- Ignorance about manipulation and its tactics can increase vulnerability since the victim is unaware of the strategies used.

Unconditional Trust:

- Unconditional trust in people can be exploited by the manipulator to gain compliance without resistance.

Self-Analysis of Personal Weaknesses

Self-analysis of personal weaknesses is a crucial step toward building a solid defense against psychological manipulation. Honestly examining one's vulnerabilities allows the development of awareness that can serve as a protective shield. Here are some key steps:

Reflection on Self-Esteem:

- Explore perceptions of oneself and work on building healthy self-esteem.

Awareness of Dependencies:

- Identify any emotional, financial, or relational dependencies and seek ways to reduce dependence.

Explore Fear of Conflict:

- Analyze how one handles the fear of conflict and develop strategies to address differences in a healthy way.

Examine the Need for Approval:

- Recognize the need for external approval and learn to build an internal foundation of trust.

Deepen Knowledge about Manipulation:

- Inform oneself about manipulation tactics to recognize them when they arise.

Develop the Ability to Say No:

- Learn to establish healthy boundaries and say no when necessary.

Seek External Support:

- Share one's vulnerabilities with trusted individuals to gain support and external perspectives.

Self-analysis requires courage and sincerity, but it is an invaluable investment in one's defense against manipulation. As we continue, we will explore strategies to strengthen resilience and protect autonomy and authenticity.

Chapter 6: Building Mental Resilience

Developing Emotional Awareness

Emotional awareness is the key to building a strong foundation of mental resilience. It means being able to recognize, understand, and manage your emotions in a healthy way. Manipulation often exploits emotions, so developing this awareness is essential for defense. Here's how:

Mindfulness and Meditation:

- Practices like mindfulness and meditation can help develop awareness of the present moment, fostering greater emotional awareness.

Explore Your Emotions:

- Take time to explore your emotions. Identify what you feel, what triggers them, and how they influence your behavior.

Keep an Emotional Journal:

- Maintain an emotional journal to track your emotions over time. This can provide insights into recurring patterns.

Practice Self-Reflection:

- Reconsider your emotional reactions to specific situations. Ask yourself the reasons behind your emotions and how you could manage them more constructively.

Seek the Guidance of a
Psychologist or Coach:

- A psychologist or coach
  can guide you in exploring
  your emotions and offer
  practical tools to manage
  them effectively.

**Empowering Self-Esteem and
Self-Confidence**

Solid self-esteem and self-
confidence are crucial for
resisting manipulation. When you
have a positive self-view, you
become less susceptible to
manipulative influence. Here's
how to enhance these qualities:

Identify and Celebrate Successes:

- Recognize your
  successes, even the
  smallest ones, and
  celebrate your
  achievements. This will
  strengthen your
  confidence in your abilities.

Address Failures with
Compassion:

- Failure is inevitable, but how you respond to failures is what matters. Treat yourself with kindness and learn from mistakes.

Set Realistic Goals:

- Set realistic goals that you can achieve. Progressive success contributes to greater self-confidence.

Cultivate Interests and Passions:

- Dedicate time to your passions. This will contribute to a sense of personal fulfillment and strengthen your self-esteem.

Practice Positive Self-Affirmation:

- Replace negative thoughts with positive affirmations about yourself. Strengthen your internal dialogue to support rather than harm your self-esteem.

Learn to Say No:

- Establish clear boundaries and learn to say no when necessary. This demonstrates self-esteem and reinforces your ability to make autonomous decisions.

Seek Positive Social Support:

- Surround yourself with people who support and inspire you. Positive social support can be a bulwark against manipulations.

Building mental resilience takes time and commitment, but it's an investment in your defense against manipulative influences. As we continue, we'll explore additional strategies to maintain mental health and protect your authenticity.

Chapter 7: Active Prevention

Strategies to Avoid Manipulative Situations

Actively preventing manipulation requires awareness and prompt action. Incorporating these strategies into your daily life can enhance your defense against manipulative influences:

Develop Critical Thinking:

- Learn to critically assess information, requests, and situations. Ask questions and seek evidence before accepting something as truth.

Set Clear Boundaries:

- Clearly define your personal and social boundaries. Don't hesitate to say no when you feel your limits are about to be crossed.

Know and Uphold Your Values:

- Affirm your values and stand firm. Being clear about your principles makes it harder for manipulators to influence you.

Learn to Recognize Emotional Manipulation:

- Familiarize yourself with emotional manipulation tactics. Recognizing exploited emotions can help you maintain mental clarity.

Strengthen the Ability to Say No:

- Be assertive in saying no when necessary. This skill is crucial to avoid getting involved in unwanted situations.

Maintain Healthy Relationships:

- Cultivate relationships based on mutual trust and respect. Positive connections can act as a shield against manipulative influences.

Monitor Your Emotional Reactions:

- Pay attention to your emotional reactions. If something seems too good to be true or elicits a strong emotional response, it could be a sign of manipulation.

Digital Awareness Education

The digital era has introduced new challenges and opportunities, and digital awareness education is crucial to prevent online manipulation. Here are some strategies:

Verify Online Sources:

- Before accepting online information, verify the source. False news is often a tool of manipulation.

Awareness of Online Scams:

- Learn to recognize online scams, including phishing schemes and fraud on social media.

Set Privacy Limits:

- Limit the amount of personal information shared online. Digital privacy is essential to avoid manipulation.

Critical Analysis of Information:

- Apply critical thinking online. Be aware of persuasive content and

digital manipulation
tactics.

Participate in Digital Education
Initiatives:

- Join digital awareness
education programs.
These initiatives provide
practical knowledge to
navigate the online world
safely.

Monitor Online Activity:

- Keep an eye on your online
activity. Digital awareness
includes an understanding
of how your online actions
can be used or
manipulated.

Create a Positive Online
Environment:

- Contribute to creating a
positive online
environment. Promote

awareness and the sharing of reliable information.

Integrating these strategies into your daily life, both online and offline, will help you build a strong and resilient defense against mental manipulation. In the next chapter, we'll explore the importance of ongoing awareness and personal growth in maintaining a resilient mind.

Chapter 8: Psychological Defenses

Techniques for Mental Defense

Developing robust psychological defenses is crucial to protect your mind from manipulation. Here are some techniques for mental defense that you can adopt:

Continuous Awareness:

- Continuous awareness of your emotions, thoughts, and behaviors forms the foundation of mental defense. Staying mindful enables you to detect any suspicious or manipulative changes.

Developing Intuition:

- Trust your intuition. If something doesn't feel right, it may not be.

Developing the ability to listen to your inner voice is crucial to counter manipulation.

Seek External Counsel:

- Talk to trusted friends, family, or mental health professionals. Obtaining external perspectives can provide a more objective view of situations.

Learn to Say "No" Safely:

- Strengthen your ability to say no. You can do it assertively and respectfully, without the need to justify yourself and without fear of retaliation.

Address Negative Emotions:

- Develop strategies to address negative emotions constructively, preventing them from being exploited by those attempting to manipulate you.

Objectively Evaluate Information:

- Before making significant decisions, take the time to objectively evaluate information. Don't let external pressures or intense emotions influence you.

Practice Self-Care:

- Take care of yourself physically, emotionally, and mentally. A healthy mind is more resilient to manipulative influences.

Set Clear Goals:

- Having clear and well-defined goals can help you stay focused and avoid being pushed in unwanted directions.

Establishing Healthy Boundaries in Relationships

Setting healthy boundaries is a crucial element in mental defense against manipulation in relationships. Here are some guidelines:

Reflect on Your Needs:

- Reflect on what is important to you and what your emotional needs are. This will help you establish boundaries in line with your requirements.

Communicate Clearly:

- Communicate your boundaries clearly and assertively to others. Be honest about what is acceptable and what is not.

Learn to Say "No":

- Learn to say no without feeling guilty. Recognize that it is your right to set limits and defend your well-being.

Be Consistent:

- Maintain consistency in your boundaries. Consistency communicates to others which behaviors are acceptable and which are not.

Recognize Manipulations:

- Be aware of manipulative tactics that might be used to cross your boundaries. Stand firm in your decisions.

Listen to Your Discomfort:

• If you feel discomfort in a situation, listen to that feeling. It could be a sign that your boundaries have been crossed.

Review and Update:

• Regularly review your boundaries based on your experiences and personal growth. Updates are a sign of authenticity and self-awareness.

The combination of strong psychological defenses and healthy boundaries in relationships creates armor against manipulative efforts. In the next chapter, we will explore the importance of learning from past episodes and growing through life experiences.

Chapter 9: Self-Analysis Tools

Guiding Questions for Exploring Your Emotions and Beliefs

Self-analysis is a profound journey into oneself, an exploration that allows a better understanding of one's emotions, thoughts, and beliefs. The following guiding questions can serve as useful tools to initiate this process of self-exploration:

What Am I Feeling Right Now?

- Start with awareness of present emotions. Identify and accept your emotions without judgment.

Which Situations Evoke Intense Emotions?

- Reflect on situations that trigger strong emotions. What is it about those

moments that deeply
affects you?

What Are My Core Values?

- Investigate the values that guide your decisions and actions. Identify what truly matters to you.

Which Beliefs Guide My Actions?

- Explore the convictions that influence your behavior. Are they based on reality, or could they be the result of limiting beliefs?

How Do I Deal with Stress and Challenges?

- Evaluate your strategies for coping with stress. Are they effective, or could they be improved?

What Do I Want to Achieve in Life?

- Ask yourself about the goals and dreams you wish to pursue. Do these reflect your vision of life and happiness?

Which Relationships Are Meaningful to Me?

- Examine your relationships. Who is important to you, and what connections do you wish to cultivate?

How Do I Handle Conflict?

- Assess your approach to conflicts. Do you have constructive ways to resolve them, or are there patterns you'd like to change?

What Are My Strengths and
Weaknesses?

- Acknowledge your talents
and areas for growth. This
will help you develop a
balanced view of yourself.

What Brings Me Happiness and
Satisfaction?

- Identify activities,
relationships, or
experiences that bring you
joy and satisfaction. How
can you include them in
your daily life?

Creating a Clear Picture of Your
Identity

Creating a clear picture of your
identity is an ongoing process of
self-exploration and reflection. In
addition to guiding questions, you
can use the following tools to
build this picture:

Personal Journal:

- Maintain a journal where you can freely express your thoughts, emotions, and daily reflections. This can be a safe space to explore your mind.

Skills and Interests Map:

- Create a map of your skills and interests. This will help you identify your passions and areas where you excel.

Emotional Family Tree:

- Build an emotional family tree of significant emotional experiences. How have they influenced who you are today?

Visual Representation of Your Identity:

- Use drawings, collages, or other visual

representations to
creatively explore your
identity.

Letter to Yourself:

- Write a letter to yourself,
reflecting on your growth,
challenges overcome, and
future goals.

External Feedback:

- Seek feedback from
trusted individuals about
your personality, skills, and
ways of facing challenges.
This can enrich your
understanding of yourself.

Mind Mapping:

- Use mind maps to
visualize connections
between your emotions,
beliefs, and experiences.

Self-analysis is a dynamic process that evolves over time. Use these tools to continue exploring your identity in a profound and constructive manner. In the next chapter, we will examine the importance of learning from past experiences to foster continuous growth.

Chapter 10: Care and Recovery

Psychological and Professional Support

Healing after manipulation requires time, commitment, and often the support of professionals. Addressing psychological wounds responsibly is crucial for care and recovery. Here are some resources and strategies:

Psychotherapy:

- Psychotherapy provides a safe space to explore and understand the experience of manipulation. Experienced therapists can offer emotional support and practical tools to address trauma.

Social Support:

- Sharing your experiences with trusted friends or family can be liberating. Strong social support helps reduce isolation and promotes connection.

Support Groups:

- Participating in support groups with people who have had similar experiences can offer understanding and shared insights. These groups can be physical or online.

Legal Counseling:

- In cases of severe manipulation, seeking legal advice may be necessary. A specialized lawyer can guide you in taking appropriate legal actions.

Mindfulness and Meditation:

- Techniques like mindfulness and meditation can help manage stress, reconnect with your body, and improve emotional well-being.

Continuous Education:

- Learning about manipulation dynamics and mental health is an important step. Knowledge provides awareness and tools to prevent future episodes.

Healing Process After Being Manipulated

The healing process is an individual journey that requires patience and self-compassion. Here are key phases of this journey:

Recognizing the Experience:

- Accepting and acknowledging the experience of manipulation is the first step. This involves validating your emotions and being aware of what happened.

Confronting Emotions:

- Exploring and confronting emotions associated with the experience is essential. Psychotherapy can be a valuable tool for this process.

Learning from Past Episodes:

- Analyzing past episodes critically. What signals did you overlook? What can you learn from these experiences to protect yourself in the future?

Establishing New Boundaries:

- Reaffirming your boundaries is crucial for the healing process. Learning to say no and defending your emotional space is a fundamental component.

Building a Support Network:

- Creating or strengthening a social support network is vital. Positive connections can be a valuable support during the healing process.

Focusing on Personal Growth:

- Using the experience as an opportunity for personal growth. This may involve learning new skills, exploring passions, or developing greater resilience.

Practicing Self-Care:

- Investing in your well-being is an act of self-compassion. The practice of healthy habits, maintaining work-life balance, and dedicating time to rest are key elements.

Seeking Legal Counseling, if Necessary:

- In severe cases, seeking legal advice can be an integral part of healing. It can bring a sense of justice and legal closure.

Healing after being manipulated is a gradual and complex process. The key is to invest time and energy in your recovery, seeking necessary support when needed. In the final chapter, we will explore the perspective of post-traumatic growth and the

possibility of emerging stronger
from the experience.

Chapter 11: The Importance of Community

How Positive Relationships Can Protect Against Manipulation

Positive relationships play a crucial role in providing emotional and social support that contributes to protection against manipulation. Here's how:

Emotional Support:

- Positive relationships offer a safe space to share emotions and concerns. Emotional support helps maintain a balanced and resilient mind.

External Perspective:

- Friends and family can provide external perspectives. This is valuable for identifying manipulative situations of which you may not be aware.

Sharing Experiences:

- Meaningful relationships allow for the sharing of experiences. Open dialogue enables learning from others' positive ways of handling similar situations.

Awareness of Behavioral Changes:

- Those close to you are often the first to notice behavioral or emotional changes. This early awareness is crucial for preventing or addressing manipulative situations.

Shared Personal Growth:

- In a supportive community, personal growth is

encouraged and shared.
This creates an
environment where
everyone is encouraged to
develop in a healthy way.

Boundary Reinforcement:

- Positive relationships
respect and reinforce
individual boundaries. This
can serve as a natural
defense against
manipulation.

Affection and Emotional
Connectivity:

- Feeling loved and
emotionally connected is
essential for mental health.
Positive relationships
provide an emotional
anchor that can protect
against external
manipulations.

The Role of Friendships and Family

Supportive Friendships:

- Friendships based on solidarity and mutual trust act as a refuge against manipulation. Cultivate bonds grounded in sincerity and shared values.

Family as a Safety Net:

- Family can be a powerful safety net. Family relationships built on trust and communication are fundamental for resilience against external manipulations.

Strengthening Family Bonds:

- Investing in strengthening family bonds creates a solid foundation for protection against manipulation. Open communication and mutual respect are key.

Common Growth:

- Family and friends can support common growth. This means facing challenges together, learning from past experiences, and growing together.

Developing Meaningful Friendships:

- Cultivating meaningful friendships involves choosing relationships based on trust, mutual growth, and reciprocal respect.

Create a Supportive Community:

- Developing a broader support community is equally important. This can include friends, family, mentors, and others who share similar values.

Strengthening Intergenerational Bonds:

- The bond between generations can provide wisdom and support. Leveraging the experience of older generations can be valuable in navigating complex situations.

Investing in positive relationships, whether friendships or family ties, builds a robust foundation that protects against manipulation. In the next chapter, we will explore the perspective of post-traumatic growth and how to transform challenging experiences into opportunities for personal development.

Chapter 12: Ethics and Social Awareness

Reflections on Personal and Social Ethics

Personal and social ethics play a fundamental role in creating healthy environments and preventing manipulation. Exploring the following reflections can contribute to developing greater ethical awareness:

Understanding Personal Values:

- Understanding your own values is the starting point for personal ethics. What principles guide your decisions and actions?

Individual Responsibility:

- Recognizing your responsibility in creating healthy relationships is a sign of ethical maturity. As an individual, what role do you play in building positive environments?

Reflection on Behaviors:

- Constant reflection on your own behaviors is crucial. Do they reflect the ethical standards you wish to promote?

Awareness of Social Impact:

- Considering the effect of your actions on the community is an important ethical element. How do your choices influence others?

Transparency and Honesty:

- Ethics involves transparency and honesty. How can you integrate these qualities into your daily interactions?

Empathy and Compassion:

- Empathy and compassion are pillars of ethics. How can you cultivate greater empathy towards others and show compassion in your actions?

Active Community Participation:

- Actively participating in your community is an ethical act. How do you contribute to the well-being of the community in which you live?

Awareness of Inequalities:

- Being aware of social inequalities is essential for robust ethics. How can you contribute to reducing disparities in your sphere of influence?

Individual Contribution to Creating Healthy Environments

Practicing Respect:

- Respect for others is a cornerstone for healthy environments. How can you show respect in your daily interactions?

Promoting Open Communication:

- Open communication is essential for creating healthy environments. How can you promote open and inclusive dialogues?

Supporting Authentic Relationships:

- Encouraging authentic relationships contributes to building healthy and trustworthy environments. How can you cultivate relationships based on genuineness?

Being a Positive Role Model:

- Being a positive role model is a significant contribution. How do your actions inspire others to behave ethically?

Addressing Injustices:

- Ethics requires the courage to address injustices. How can you advocate for fairness and justice in your community?

Cultivating a Supportive Environment:

- Creating a supportive environment is a notable contribution. How can you support the well-being of others and cultivate a culture of mutual support?

Being Aware of Your Actions:

- Awareness of your actions is crucial. How can you be more aware of the consequences of your choices?

Embracing Diversity:

- Inclusion is a sign of a healthy environment. How can you embrace and celebrate diversity in your interactions?

Conclusions on Ethical and Social Awareness

Ethical and social awareness is a continuous process of self-reflection and conscious action. Recognizing your impact and contributing to creating healthy environments is an act of responsibility and a step towards a more equitable and supportive society. In the conclusion, we will explore the theme of post-traumatic growth and how to transform challenges into opportunities for personal development.

Chapter 13: Looking Toward the Future

An Optimistic View of Life After the Experience of Manipulation

Looking toward the future with optimism is a significant step in the healing and personal growth process after experiencing manipulation. Here are some positive perspectives to consider:

Personal Rebirth:

- After the darkness of manipulation, the opportunity for personal rebirth arises. This period marks a new phase of your life, characterized by awareness, strength, and growth.

Learning and Growth:

- Looking toward the future involves learning from past

experiences. Every challenge is an opportunity for learning, and personal growth emerges from assimilating these lessons.

Cultivating Meaningful Relationships:

- After a period of manipulation, building relationships based on trust and reciprocity becomes a priority. Looking toward the future means cultivating authentic and meaningful connections.

-

Restoring Self-Trust:

- An optimistic view of the future involves restoring self-trust. Recognizing your inner strength is essential for facing challenges that may arise along the way.

Renewing Goals and Dreams:

- Looking toward the future involves renewing goals and dreams. This may mean reconsidering priorities and charting new paths in line with your personal growth.

Cultivating Gratitude:

- Gratitude is a lens through which to view the future with optimism. Recognizing positive aspects of your life contributes to maintaining a positive perspective.

Embracing Change:

- Looking toward the future requires the ability to embrace change. Mental flexibility and a willingness to adapt are key to building a satisfying future.

Continuous Development of Mental Resilience

Accepting Vulnerability:

- Mental resilience develops by accepting one's vulnerability. Being open and honest about your challenges contributes to building a strong foundation.

Cultivating an Optimistic Mindset:

- An optimistic mindset fosters resilience. Seeing challenges as opportunities for growth rather than obstacles promotes a positive perspective.

Supporting Your Emotions:

- Resilience involves the ability to manage emotions healthily. Being aware of your emotional reactions and developing strategies to address them is crucial.

Learning from Adversity:

- Every experience, even a difficult one, offers valuable lessons. Mental resilience develops by learning from adversity and applying these lessons to the future.

Cultivating Support Networks:

- Having strong support networks is crucial for mental resilience. Cultivating positive relationships provides the necessary support during challenging times.

Flexibility in Problem-Solving:

- Being flexible in problem-solving is a key characteristic of resilience. Adapting to changing circumstances and finding creative solutions contributes to mental strength.

Focus on Controllable Aspects:

- Mental resilience develops by focusing on controllable aspects. Concentrating on what can be changed helps maintain a sense of personal power.

Conclusion: Looking to the Future with Confidence

Looking to the future with confidence requires a continuous commitment to personal growth and mental resilience. Facing the experience of manipulation is a challenging journey, but it can become fertile ground where inner strength and awareness flourish. Through a positive lens, the vision of the future becomes a path of possibilities, growth, and personal fulfillment. In the final conclusion, we will explore the concept of post-traumatic growth and how to transform challenges into opportunities for a richer and more meaningful life.

Conclusion: A New Beginning

Throughout the pages of this book dedicated to understanding and defending against mental manipulation, we have explored a broad spectrum of topics essential for psychological well-being and personal growth. Let's briefly recap the main points covered:

Summary of Key Points Covered:

Introduction to Mental Manipulation:

- Contextualizing the importance of the theme, we examined the devastating effects of mental manipulation and the urgent need to address this widespread phenomenon.

Understanding Mental Manipulation:

- We explored definitions and types of mental manipulation, analyzing the complex psychological mechanisms involved.

Early Signs of Manipulation:

- Focusing on early signs, we learned to recognize manipulative behaviors and identify potentially risky situations.

The Psychology of the Manipulator:

- We investigated the psychological profile of those who practice manipulation, exploring motivations and power dynamics.

Individual Vulnerability:

- Analyzing factors that increase vulnerability to manipulation, we encouraged self-analysis of personal weaknesses.

Building Mental Resilience:

- Strategies for developing emotional awareness, enhancing self-esteem, and self-confidence took shape.

Active Prevention:

- We explored strategies to avoid manipulation situations and emphasized the importance of digital and psychological awareness education.

Psychological Defenses:

- Mental defense techniques and the importance of

establishing healthy boundaries in relationships were discussed to promote conscious defense.

Tools for Self-Analysis:

- We provided guided questions to explore emotions and beliefs, helping to create a clear picture of one's identity.

Care and Recovery:

- The importance of psychological and professional support was highlighted, along with the healing process after manipulation.

The Importance of Community:

- Reflections on the contribution of positive relationships and the fundamental role of friendships and family in preventing manipulation took shape.

Ethics and Social Awareness:

- We pondered personal and social ethics, exploring how individual contributions can create healthy environments and prevent manipulation.

Looking Toward the Future:

- Finally, we explored an optimistic view of life after the experience of manipulation and the ongoing development of mental resilience.

Call to Action and Knowledge Sharing:

Each chapter of this book was designed to provide not only knowledge but also practical tools to address mental manipulation and cultivate a resilient mind.

Now, the call to action is directed to you, the reader:

Share Knowledge:

- Share what you have learned with others. Knowledge sharing is a crucial step in creating awareness and preventing manipulation.

Cultivate Healthy Relationships:

- Apply teachings on early signs, the psychology of the manipulator, and creating healthy environments to cultivate meaningful relationships in your life.

Promote Awareness Education:

- Contribute to the promotion of digital and psychological awareness education in your community, thereby contributing to a more aware society.

Develop Your Mental Resilience:

*   Utilize the tools provided to develop and strengthen your mental resilience. Face challenges with courage, learn, and grow from the experience.

In conclusion, we remember that mental manipulation can be defeated through awareness, knowledge, and action. We look to the future with confidence, knowing that every step toward awareness is a step toward mental freedom and personal growth.

May this book be your guiding light toward a more conscious, resilient, and possibility-filled life.

www.ingramcontent.com/pod-product-compliance
Lightning Source LLC
Chambersburg PA
CBHW031318250726

48656CB00005B/1862